TEACHING
CIVIL RIGHTS
-VOTING RIGHTS-

By: Ronnie K. Barnes

VOTE

UNITED STATES OF AMERICA

Illustrated by: Obayomi Israel Olamide

Boynton Street is named after me and my husband S.W. Boynton in Selma Alabama and I have a street named after myself Amelia Boynton Robinson Parkway in Tuskegee, Alabama.

"A Voteless People Is A Hopeless People"

ISBN: 978-1-735-4442-4-6

Illustrator: Obayomi Israel Olamide

Ronnie K Barnes: visit my website at Ronniethewriterweaver.com
RKBarnes0824@gmail.com
RKBarnes0824@hotmail.com

DEDICATION

This book is written for all the world's children: black, brown white, yellow to enlighten them about the past and how far we have progressed into the 21st century.

I also show homage in honoring Amelia Boynton Robinson and her husband S. W. Boynton for their work modeling the Voting Rights Movement and Civil Rights Movement as early as the latter part of the 1920s.

This children's book is a guide for youngsters from the ages 7-13 to learn about 1965 Voting Rights Movement history: It represents some of the life works of Amelia Boynton Robinson and her husband S.W. Boynton and teachable lessons for children to be taught from illustrations throughout the book.

Amelia Boynton Robinson Teaches Voting Rights and Civil Rights encourages and challenges children to learn about the Voting Rights and Civil Rights Struggles of the 1960s moving forward into the 21st Century.

Amelia Boynton Robionson home located at 1315 Lapsley Street is where Amelia Boynton Robinson along with the Reverend Dr. Martin Luther King Jr. and several United States congressmen produced the first draft of the Voting rights Act in 1965 on Amelia's kitchen table.

GO TO HIGH SCHOOL GO TO COLLEGE

My name is Amelia Boynton.

I am known as the "Mother of Voting Rights Movement" while others know me as the Matriarch of the Voting Rights Movement.

My early childhood life: I was introduced to politics. I remember riding about with my mother on the horse and buggy in Savannah, Georgia in 1921 at the age of 10 years old.

I knock on doors passing out flyers to register and vote. I also would ask the question are you a registered voter if not, why not? If registered, did you vote?

I knocked on doors in 1921 giving women information to register to vote after the 19th Amendment gave women the right to vote.

My mother and I carried women to the polls to cast their votes by horse, buggy and carriage.

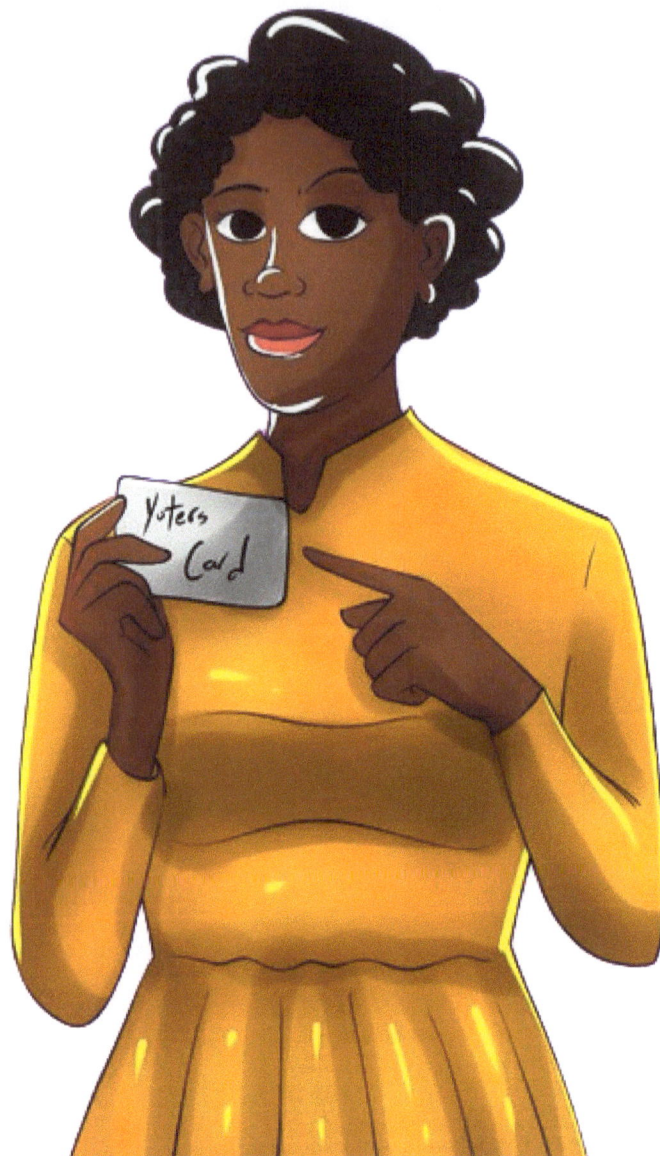

When I came of age, I registered to vote.

Young Amelia: I was born to be a leader.

College Graduate: Amelia graduated from the Tuskegee Institute. She became very good friends with her professor, George Washington Carver.

School Teacher: Amelia Boynton Robinson, I am known for teaching children about the 1965 Voting Rights Movement in Selma, Alabama. I also taught my students the importance of registering to vote once turning 18 years old.

"A VOTELESS PEOPLE IS A HOPELESS PEOPLE"

In the 1940s and 1960s S.W. Boynton and his wife Amelia owned a business that offered real estate, employment service and life insurance on the inside above the door entrance was a sign which read: "A Voteless People is a Hopeless People."

1315 Lapsley Street located in Selma, Alabama was the home of S.W. and his wife Amelia Boynton.

The Boynton's Home became popular during the [Voting Rights] movement.
Many voting rights events like sit-ins, marches, campaigns, protests, and numerous other events were planned at the Boynton's home.

1315 Lapsley Street is where Amelia, the Rev. Dr. Martin Luther King Jr., and several United States Congressman would meet up to produce the first draft of the Voting Rights Act in 1965 on Mrs. Boynton's kitchen table.

Amelia: In 1964 I became the 1st Black woman to run for United States Congress in Alabama.

I received 10 percent of the votes at a time when only 2 percent of the voting population was made up of African Americans.

Brown Chapel A.M.E. Church is located in Selma, Alabama. Today, it is known as the Mecca for the voting rights movement. A major role in the rally and protest events were held here at the church.

Brown Chapel A.M.E Church is now a historical landmark located at 410 Martin Luther King Jr. Boulevard in Selma, Alabama and it was a starting point for the march from Selma to Montgomery Alabama in 1965.

It was also one of the meeting places and office locations for the Southern Christian Leadership Conference (SCLC) during the Selma Movement.

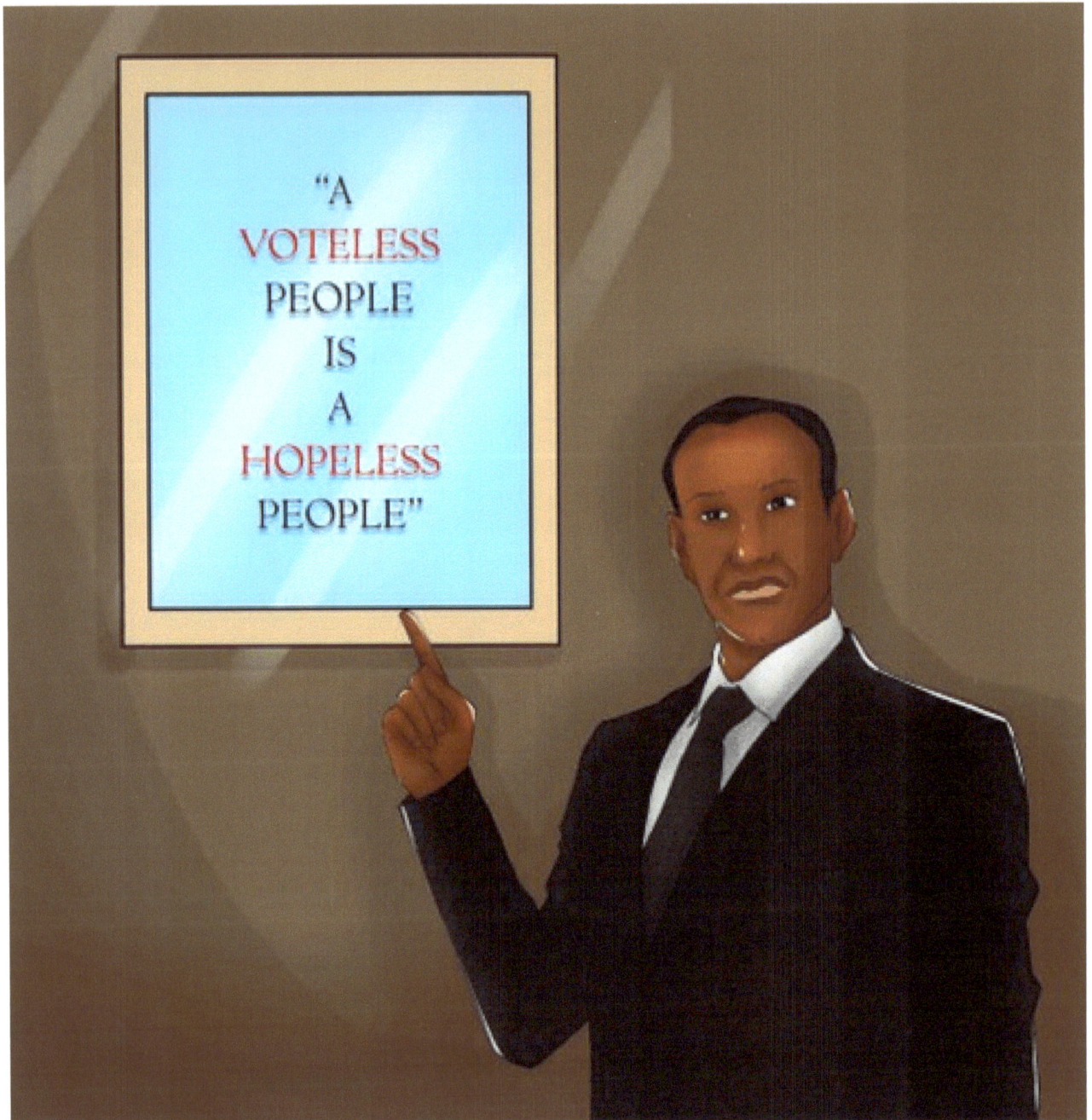

The first question my husband S.W. Boynton would ask anyone who stepped into our place of business in Selma, Alabama, were "Are you a registered voter?" "If not, why aren't you?" He would then say to them "A Voteless People Is A Hopeless People."

Edmund Pettus Bridge, a bridge crossing the Alabama River in Selma, Alabama. This site became known as "Bloody Sunday," a landmark event in the history of the American Civil Rights Movement.

On that day, March 7, 1965, white law-enforcement officers violently removed protesters, the biggest majority of whom were African Americans as they crossed the bridge during the first attempt to initiate the Selma March.

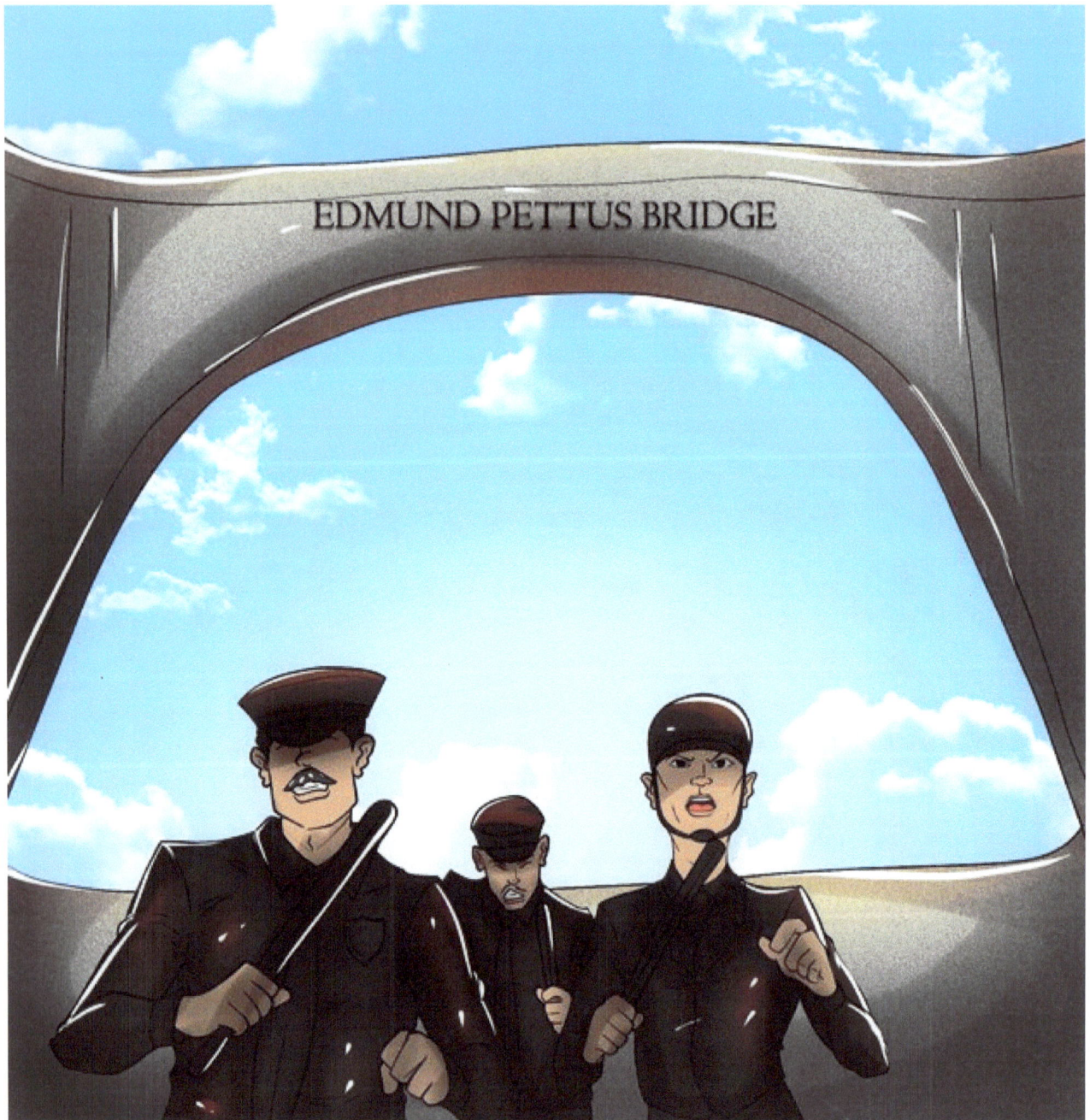

Amelia describes what she saw first hand as a citizen looking on as a marcher:
"They were standing erect, they were dressed in their uniform, they had clubs, they had cattle prod—one in one hand, and one in the other."

Amelia: I Was beaten down by the trooper. He forcefully clubbed me over and over again across my neck, back, and shoulders, and then he shot tear gas directly into my face causing me to collapse and fall to the ground unconscious.

On March 7, 2015, during the 50th anniversary of "Bloody Sunday", President Barack Obama walked hand in hand with Amelia Boynton Robinson across that very bridge where she was beaten down and left for dead.

A resident of Montgomery, Alabama, Ronnie Kennedy Barnes holds a bachelor degree in public relations from the University of Alabama, Tuscaloosa Alabama and master degree in human resource management from Troy University (Montgomery, Alabama Campus). He is an US Army veteran and a former newspaper reporter, and he has spent twenty-five years as a government employee. He is also a Master Mason Prince Hall Affiliation, and he is a member of Alpha Phi Alpha Fraternity Incorporated and Beta Alpha Gamma Christian Fraternity.

Barnes has authored and written Amelia Boynton Robinson, Matriarch of Voting Rights Movement. He has also authored Amelia 1965 Old Battles Become New Again Voting Rights-Civil Rights 2nd Edition: Amelia Boynton Robinson Teaches Voting Rights Civil Rights, children's book, 60th Anniversary Commemoration Edition Selma to Montgomery March Amelia Boynton Robinson Mother Of The Voting Rights Movement Book of Quotes and the book titled The New Joyful Sounds, A Portrait of Gospel Music and the Melody. Barnes has also published several journals and teacher's monthly planners, masonic and eastern star journals, and password tracker books.

A NOTE FROM THE AUTHOR

This book will help children to learn about
Amelia Boynton Robinson legacy and the critical role she
played in giving the nation the right to vote. Amelia Boynton
Robinson is known as the Matriarch of the Voting Rights
Movement whereas to others she's called the Mother of the
Voting Rights Movement.

It is my hope that children between the ages of 7-13 will learn
about voting rights and the civil rights movement and the
strength, pride, and courage it took for Amelia Boynton
Robinson to stand up and fight for those rights for all mankind.

The Voting Rights Act signed into law on August 6, 1965 was
a victory for the Civil Rights Movement, particularly African
Americans [Black people] and equal rights for all people.

On August 6, 1965, after the march from Selma Alabama to
Montgomery Alabama The United States of America
President Lyndon B. Johnson signed the federal Voting Rights
Act into law.

Amelia Boynton Robinson was invited to the ceremony at the
White House as a guest of honor for President Lyndon B.
Johnson.

AMELIA'S TEACHES CHILDREN TO REMEMBER:

1. Be proud of yourself.
2. Develop those potentials and say this: I know I can be what I want to be if I put my mind to believing I can achieve and do it.
3. Have self respect, have race pride and believe nothing can stop me from going to the top.
4. Self-Esteem is very important, "Love Yourself."

Ronnie K Barnes has authored several books: Amelia Boynton Robinson Matriarch Of The Voting Rights Movement, Amelia 1965 Old Battles Battles Become New Again Voting Rights-Civil Rights, 60 Years Commemoration Edition Selma to Montgomery Alabama March Amelia Boynton Robinson Mother Of The Voting Rights Movement. He is a graduate of Troy State University (Montgomery, Alabama Campus) where he earned a Master Degree in Human Resource Management.

www.ingramcontent.com/pod-product-compliance
Lightning Source LLC
Chambersburg PA
CBHW061051090426

42740CB00002B/114